DISCOVER LANDSCAPES

Bea

Lake District

Val Corbett

MYRIAD
LONDON

Central Lake District

The heart of the Lake District contains many of the important towns of the region such as Windermere, Bowness and Ambleside. Its stunning scenery has been a source of wonder and inspiration to artists and writers over the generations. William Wordsworth went to school in Hawkshead and spent most of his adult life at Grasmere and Rydal Mount. Pretty villages such as Ambleside, Chapel Stile and Troutbeck abound and close at hand is the Langdale valley with its unusual and spectacular rock-topped "pikes".

Windermere *above and left*

The month of September is perfect for enjoying the drifting beauty of the autumn mist that lies over the lakes. The view (above) looks south over Windermere and was taken at dawn from the lower slopes of Loughrigg Fell. Windermere is the longest of all the lakes in the Lake District, and the largest lake in England.

Windermere is the only town in the Lake District fully accessible by rail – in fact, the town developed thanks to the construction of the railway line which was built in 1848. Just off the main road, Queen Adelaide's Hill, on the eastern shore of the lake, gives wonderful views of Windermere and the surrounding fells. There are also spectacular viewpoints across the lake from Biskey Howe, School Knott and Orrest Head – a view made popular by the poet William Wordsworth.

Blackwell House *above*

One of Britain's most important Arts & Crafts houses lies just a mile south of Bowness. The house occupies a stunning position overlooking Windermere and was designed as a holiday home by MH Baillie Scott for the Manchester brewer Sir Edward Holt. Baillie Scott who, along with John Ruskin and William Morris, was one of the major exponents of the Arts & Crafts movement of the late 19th century, built the house in the Manorial Style promoted by William Morris. Today the restored house is open to the public and contains an impressive collection of period furniture, paintings, sculpture and ceramics.

Troutbeck *below*

The village of Troutbeck stretches for more than a mile along a side road off the Kirkstone Pass that links Windermere and Ullswater. It contains many wonderful examples of attractive Lake District architecture including pubs and pretty stone cottages. The famous Townend House (owned by the National Trust) is at the southern end of the village. A good example of a wealthy farmer's house, it dates from the 17th century. The village church, unusually just called "Jesus Christ", has a window by Burne-Jones and a churchyard filled with a cheery mass of daffodils in spring. For many years Troutbeck was the centre of the greatest of the annual hound-trailing meetings held throughout the Lake District. The hounds pursued a pre-laid scent up the peaks through torrents and over drystone walls. Thousands of spectators would descend on Troutbeck to view this dramatic scene.

Ambleside *above, right and below*

The village of Ambleside developed next to Stock Beck, whose fast-flowing waters powe the local watermills. Traces of this history can be seen all around the town. The Water Wheel Shop is a converted mill and still has an intact waterwheel on the outside of the building together with some pieces of machinery inside.

The commanding 180ft (55m) spire of St Mary's church dominates the town. The chu was built in 1854 to a design by Sir George Gilbert Scott, the architect made famous by London buildings including St Pancras station and the Albert Memorial. The famous Lake poet William Wordsworth had his office in the town when he was distributor of stamps Westmorland. He is commemorated, together with his wife and sister, by a memorial ch and stained-glass window. St Mary's also boasts a handsome mural depicting the ancient rush-bearing ceremony in which parishioners once covered the church floors with fresh rushes every summer.

Surrounded by beautiful mountain scenery, Ambleside lies on the main road that run between Keswick and Kendal. Much more than a village – it even has its own cinema – Ambleside has a thriving student community at St Martin's College, and hosts the Lake District summer music festival. The oldest part of the town, the route up to the Kirksto Pass, has some attractive old houses and streets. Peggy Hill, off North Road and sharply uphill from Stock Bridge, is a good place to start exploring. Dating from the 17th centur Bridge House (right) on Rydal Road is a National Trust property. Originally a summer h

Ambleside Hall, the building straddles Stock Beck. Beyond it are the old mill buildings complete with [wate]rwheel, which is now a restaurant. In the mid 19th century this tiny building was home to the Rigg [famil]y – mother, father and six children. In 1926 the house was purchased by local people for a sum of [£100?] and donated to the National Trust who used it as their first information office.

Waterhead attractions

The pier at Waterhead was established in 1845 at the most northerly point of Windermere. Passengers often alight at the pier surprised to find that it is almost a mile away from the town of Ambleside, which may explain why a horse-drawn carriage does good trade, carrying passengers between the ferry and the town. Waterhead is a busy ferry terminal: steamers and launches sail all year round to Bowness and Lakeside. It is also possible to hire a rowing boat at the pier. Nearby, Borrans Park is a tranquil spot overlooking the lake with the remains of the important Roman fort, Galava, still visible nearby. This fort was one of a chain built by the Emperor Hadrian to protect trade routes in Cumbria. A Roman road linked Galava with the fort at Hardknott and the harbour at Ravenglass.

Dove Cottage, Grasmere *above*

At the very heart of the Lake District, just off the main road from Ambleside to Keswick, Grasmere is famous as the home of William Wordsworth for the most creative period of his life. The poet lived at Dove Cottage and its tiny rooms are still much as they would have been when he lived there with his sister, Dorothy, and wife, Mary. The life of the poet, his family and their many visitors is brilliantly described by Dorothy in her diaries. William, Dorothy and Mary were all buried in the church of St Oswald and their graves are a place of pilgrimage for lovers of the Lakeland Poets.

Looking across the lake from one of the shingle beaches on the southern shore (below right) you can see the white face of the Prince of Wales Hotel on the far side. Dove Cottage is just tucked behind to the right. The view shows Helm Crag to the left, the Pass of Dunmail Raise and the soaring slopes of Seat Sandal.

Rydal Mount *above*

Rydal is best-known for its association with William Wordsworth. Rydal Mount, one of several characterful houses in the village, was the poet's home for the last four decades of his life, from 1813 to his death in 1850. In contrast to the simplicity of Dove Cottage, Rydal Mount was grand and spacious. In 1969 the poet's great-great granddaughter Mary Henderson acquired the property. The house has been open to the public since 1970 and remains in the ownership of the Wordsworth family. It contains beautiful furniture, together with family possessions and portraits. The gardens are laid out as they were when the poet was in residence and visitors can see his "writing hut" which overlooks the grounds and two nearby lakes.

Elterwater *left*

Four miles west of Ambleside, the much-visited little village of Elterwater is scenically placed at the entrance to the Langdale valley and shares its name with the adjacent small lake. The first view of the village, coming either from Grasmere or Ambleside, is always impressive with the Coniston Fells and Langdale Pikes forming a dramatic background.

The village was formerly industrial, and its pretty little slate cottages were built for the workers at the nearby Kirkstone slate quarries. A walking route to Little Langdale takes in views of old and new slate quarries. Later a gunpowder manufacturing business brought workers to the village. The Britannia Inn, with its low ceilings and slate floors, is the focal point of the village. Elterwater is the smallest of the 16 lakes in the Lake District. "Elter" is the Norse word for swan, so Elterwater literally means "Swan Lake". Whooper swans regularly migrate to the lake in winter from Iceland.

Chapel Stile *below*

The tiny village of Chapel Stile is the kind of place where it seems perfectly normal to meet sheep walking along the middle of the village street or grazing the verge. The sturdy church, with its fortified tower, serves the whole of Langdale and is a fine sight rising above the village with Silver Howe as a backdrop. The Cumbria Way long-distance footpath enjoys the same view as it passes the village. Slate quarrying, both past and present, is evident everywhere: the scree on the fellside, the occasional boom of quarry blasting and the village houses themselves which are almost all built of slate.

Grasmere attractions

Just off the main road from Ambleside to Keswick, Grasmere is in the very heart of the Lake District and is at the centre of some of Lakeland's most beautiful landscapes.

The village is home to the famous gingerbread shop (below) which lies close to one of the entrances to the churchyard at St Oswald's. The gingerbread, which is more like a deliciously spicy shortbread than cake, comes from an original recipe created by a local woman, Sarah Nelson, and is sold from the tiny cottage on the edge of the churchyard of St Oswald's. This cottage was the village school for more than 200 years, and William Wordsworth, his wife and sister all taught there.

A few miles south-east of Grasmere, close to Wordsworth's last home at Rydal Mount, stands the imposing 17th-century house, Rydal Hall (below centre). Now owned by the Diocese of Carlisle and used as a conference and retreat centre, the beautiful formal gardens are open to the public with a little cafe nearby.

Wordsworth's church

The ancient church of St Oswald (left), where Wordsworth worshipped, is at the heart of Grasmere. The poet planted eight yew trees in the churchyard, and one of them marks the grave of him and his wife, Mary. His sister Dorothy and his children are buried nearby. The commemorative family gravestone (above) is close by.

Wordsworth and Potter at Hawkshead

The poet and his brother John were both pupils at the old Hawkshead grammar school, founded in 1585. William's desk at the grammar school, covered in carvings done by the boys, can be seen in the school-house which is now a museum. As a boy, Wordsworth lodged in the cottage of Anne Tyson (below), at nearby Colthouse. Anne is reputed to have had a great influence on him: she was a gifted storyteller and may have sparked an interest in tales of the countryside in the young poet.

Hawkshead is also the home of the Beatrix Potter Gallery, a 17th-century building which was once the office of a local solicitor, William Heelis, who married the author in 1913. Now owned by the National Trust, the building has changed little over the years. It houses a changing exhibition of Beatrix Potter's original drawings and illustrations.

wkshead

ay between Windermere and
rthern end of Coniston Water,
mous village lies just north of
aite Water. It is a compact
of picturesque whitewashed
ngs, dominated by the church
Michael's and All Angels (above)
ts position high above the
on Hawkshead Hill.
earby lies the ever-popular
y spot of Tarn Hows (left).
here there are views towards
elvellyn range, Weatherlam and
ngdale Pikes. A one-and-a-half
ootpath runs around the tarn.

The Langdales

The Langdales consist of two valleys – Great Langdale and Little Langdale, which join at Elterwater. They are famous for dramatic and varied scenery, and are home to the rocky-topped Langdale Pikes.

Great Langdale (right) is dominated by the Langdale Pikes which rise abruptly from the level valley floor. The area abounds in colourful names – the Pikes themselves are Pike O'Stickle and Harrison Stickle on the right, while further right is Pavey Arc, Lakeland's biggest cliff, which is cut through by Jack's Rake, a wonderfully challenging trail. Beneath is the sombrely named Dungeon Ghyll and to the left are Crinkle Crags and Bow Fell.

The slopes around Little Langdale Tarn (below) are bathed in early morning November sun with the huge bulk of Weatherlam behind. This valley retains its traditional character, and only light traffic uses the narrow road to Wrynose Pass. The tarn itself is inaccessible by road but a popular footpath passes over the picturesque little stone Slaters Bridge which crosses the infant river Brathay soon after it leaves the tarn.

Southern Lake District

This region is a fascinating blend, from the "classic" Lakeland scenery of southern Windermere and Coniston to the pretty villages situated in lush countryside overlooking Morecambe Bay. A visit to Beatrix Potter's house at Hill Top is a must for everyone who has enjoyed her books and you can identify some of the scenes in the surrounding hills and fields which inspired her illustrations. Coniston is packed with historical references – its many disused mines, Brantwood, the lakeshore home of John Ruskin, and the memorials to Donald Campbell.

Coniston *right*

On a still September morning the peaks of the Old Man of Coniston and Weatherlam towering above the village of Coniston are reflected on the calm surface of Coniston Water. This view from Brantwood, the home of the critic and social reformer John Ruskin, was considered by him to be the finest in the Lake District. Further up the lake Arthur Ransome enjoyed a similar view while he was writing *Swallows and Amazons* and High Bank Ground, the farm in the foreground, was the setting for the book. Brantwood is perched on a narrow shelf at the foot of a steep fell high above Coniston Water. The John Ruskin museum in the town was established as a memorial to Ruskin and as a celebration of the area's heritage. The museum also honours the life of Donald Campbell, who perished on the lake in an attempt to break the world water-speed record. His gravestone, in the shape of his boat *Bluebird*, can be seen in Coniston's new cemetery.

Beatrix Potter's House *above*

The villages of Near and Far Sawrey lie one mile apart between Windermere and Esthwaite Water. Hill Top, the home of Beatrix Potter, is situated in Near Sawrey. The house, now owned by the National Trust, is open to the public. The author's furniture, china and watercolours are on display. In the kitchen garden there are delightful litle tableaux, reminiscent of scenes from *Peter Rabbit*. Beatrix Potter purchased the house in 1905 with the royalties from the sales of her first few books written in London but inspired by regular visits to the Lake District. Hill Top soon became her home and in 1909 she also bought the adjoining Castle Farm which then became the home where she wrote and managed her farms.

Kelly Hall Tarn *right*

This quiet stretch of water lies only a short distance from the road running up the west side of Coniston Water. In the background are some of the Coniston Fells including Dow Crag and the Old Man.

Lakeside *below*

One mile north of Newby Bridge, this popular spot on Windermere is busy with steam trains and pleasurecraft. The station platform and landing stages at Lakeside can be seen above the mass of hawthorn blossom on the slopes of Gummers How. Steam trains puff up and down the scenic little railway line which follows the river Leven for just over three miles from Haverthwaite. A popular way of extending the trip is to then board one of the boats run by Windermere Lake Cruises. In summer, an alternative is to take a little ferry crossing the lake to Fellfoot Park and Garden, owned by the National Trust. This is the perfect spot for a picnic, a visit to the tea room, or a wander around the Victorian gardens and along the lake shore. The Aquatarium at Lakeside is a popular choice for families – you can be nose to nose with fish and then walk in a tunnel beneath them.

Cartmel Priory church *above*

The picturesque village of Cartmel lies two miles west of Grange-over-Sands on the southern edge of the Lake District, on a small peninsula jutting into the flat expanse of Morecambe Bay. The Church of St Mary and St Michael (Cartmel Priory church), founded in 1188, towers over the village.

Crosthwaite church *left*

The attractive village church of St Mary's, Crosthwaite, was built in 1878. The name of the village means "a cross in a clearing" which may derive from a former chapel. The church is situated next to the pub, The Punch Bowl, which dates from the 17th century. In late April the Lyth and Winster valleys are awash with the white blossom of damson trees in the little orchards scattered around the area. The warm, sheltered climate of southern Lakeland is ideal for growing damsons and each spring the Westmorland damson association holds a "damson day" at Howe, near Crosthwaite.

Eastern Lake District

This area is dominated by the Helvellyn range and by two lakes, the narrow but picturesque Ullswater and the bleak Haweswater Reservoir. The high fells contain some of the Lake District's best-known mountain scenery: the steep-sided Striding Edge, Patterdale, Kirkstone Pass (Lakeland's highest mountain road) and the Roman road on High Street. The villages of Pooley Bridge and Glenridding at either end of Ullswater are ideal stopping off places for visitors wishing to explore this diverse and picturesque area. Ullswater stretches for nine miles and makes an elongated "z" shape, giving it three separate reaches of water.

Lanty's Tarn *above*

A short, sharp climb from the main car park in Glenridding leads to the lovely, shallow Lanty's Tarn. This fairytale stretch of water was named after Lancelot Dobson who owned most of Grisedale. His house, just below the tarn, is now in ruins. Close by is the little knoll of Keldas. From its summit there is a wonderful view across Ullswater almost perfectly framed by Scots pine. A round walk from Glenridding to Fairfield, via St Sunday Crag and returning via Grisedale, takes you past the tarn which was built to supply water to Patterdale Hall, in the valley below.

Glencoyne Farm *right*

The fat chimneystacks that poke up from the roof of the white-painted farmhouse overlooking Ullswater are typical of old lakeland farmhouses. There are two theories as to why the stacks were round: one that their shape was better for drawing smoke, the other that, "square ones are better for the devil to hide in". This view is from the path to the former miners' cottages at Seldom Seen, in Glencoynedale. It was a favourite of Queen Victoria, and she may well have been amused had she known that it would be so little changed well over a century later.

Striding Edge *above*

The route up to Helvellyn is one of the most popular walks in the Lake District. In the summer there are often hundreds of walkers making their way to and from the summit. At the top, Helvellyn is grassy and remarkably flat, but at the eastern side of the fell lies the knife-sharp ridge of Striding Edge. The narrow path along its top has great drops on either side and can be dangerous. Near the top of the mountain is the Gough Memorial which commemorates the death of Charles Gough, a lakeland tourist who, in 1805, died whilst trying to cross Striding Edge. His dog guarded his body for three months, before he and his master's corpse were discovered.

Ullswater boathouse *left*

Anglers and photographers are generally the only people to be found on the shoreline of the lake, enjoying the dawn, where early mist, which gathers across the lake, dissolves gently as the sun rises. This view of the much photographed Pooley Bridge boathouse looks across to Arthur's Pike and Bonscale Pike, both good spots for a quiet fell walk.

Angle Tarn *above*

Not to be confused with the stretch of water of the [same]
name under Bowfell, Angle Tarn lies high above Patter[dale]
and Hartsop. The tarn has a gentler appearance than [most]
other high level lakes since it is attractively cupped by [the]
surrounding crags and is unusually indented and reedy[. In]
the far distance are the more northerly stretches of t[he]
Helvellyn range. The route of the coast-to-coast walk
passes close by.

Haweswater *below* and High Street

This stretch of water is a reservoir created in the 19[20s.]
It has a peaceful air, but submerged beneath the wate[r is]
the old village of Mardale, drowned when the valley w[as]
flooded. A wall runs along the 28-mile length of High
Street, the course of a Roman road.

Pooley Bridge *above*

This bustling village lies close to the northern tip of Ullswater, where the river Eamont leaves the lake, about five miles south of Penrith. Until recently Pooley Bridge was a quiet backwater; now it bustles with visitors and sometimes feels as if it is in danger of being swamped. The narrowness of the old bridge, built for horses and carts, causes occasional log jams as cars try to cross at the height of the summer. King John granted the fishing village its charter in the 12th century. On the market square stands an unusual millennium monument consisting of a sandstone pillar topped by a weather vane and a fish. The Ullswater Steamer Company boats link Pooley Bridge with Howtown and Glenridding and connect with excellent walks on the eastern side of the lake.

Northern Lake District

The lively town of Keswick is the largest in the Lake District. It is sited on the northern shores of Derwent Water whose stunning scenery and boating attractions make this easily the most popular destination for visitors to the Northern Lakes. Along with Keswick, this area is packed with other scenic treasures. Bassenthwaite and the three adjoining lakes of Buttermere, Crummock Water and Loweswater are all surrounded by stunning fells with a scattering of characterful and pretty villages. Literary and historic associations abound, particularly in the remote valleys of Borrowdale and Buttermere.

Derwent Water

Located beneath the fells of Cat Bells and Skiddaw, Derwent Water is one of the larger of the lakes in the region – at its widest point it is just over a mile wide. The view (above) is from the peak of Cat Bells with the massive bulk of Skiddaw and Blencathra looming in the distance. The little hill of Castlehead, close to Keswick, provides a view (left) across the town to the west towards Cat Bells and Causey Pike. The first snows of winter (below) coat the summit of Skiddaw, seen here in the distance across Derwent Water. The traditional teak launches operate a frequent service, which is very useful as the 12-mile circuit can be too much for inexperienced walkers.

Around Keswick

The Moot Hall (far left), which dates from 1813, is Keswick's best known landmark. It houses the tourist information centre and, at its west end, is the famous "one-handed clock". In the past the hall served as a courthouse, a museum, a prison and a local market. The bell in the tower bears the date 1601 and the letters HDRO. It is thought that this came from the ancestral home of the Derwentwater family on Lord's Isle.

From the boat landings it is possible to hire a rowing boat or take one of the many pleasure trips around the lake. There are splendid views of Cat Bells, Skiddaw and the many islands that grace Derwent Water including St Herbert's Island and Lord's Island, both of which are owned by the National Trust.

Castlerigg *right*

Dating from around 3000BC, the Castlerigg stone circle sits in a natural amphitheatre of hills, with panoramic views of the fells. It is thought that the circle originally consisted of 70 stones. Today there are 38 stones which form a rough oval, within which there is an unusual small rectangular setting of another 10 stones. Little is known about its origins although many have speculated that it may have been an astronomical observatory and a place for meeting and trading. When snow is on the ground the circle takes on an other worldly air and the surrounding mountains, including Blencthra, seem to crowd in around the stones.

Borrowdale

Stretching from the head of Derwent Water south to Seathwaite, Borrowdale is walled in by steep crags on all sides. The tiny village of Grange-in-Borrowdale (right) is near the southern end of the lake. A short distance upstream the "jaws of Borrowdale" leave just enough room for the road and river to snake through. The low-slung twin arches of Grange Bridge (below) span the two branches of the river Derwent that flow either side of a small island, a popular spot for children to play on a summer's day. Most buildings in the area are constructed from green slate and the slate, pebbles and stones that line the riverbed give the clear water a striking blue-green translucence. The Church of the Holy Trinity in the village has an unexpected barrel-shaped ceiling, finished with an unusual saw-tooth design.

Ashness Bridge *left*

Taken on a morning in February, ice has formed on the rocks of Barrow Beck which flows under this ancient packhorse bridge on the road to Watendlath. This is one of the Lake District's treasured views and is photographed by literally thousands of people every year. From here the lake is only visible in the far distance; rising behind it is the Skiddaw massif, partially topped with snow.

In the days before motor transport, packhorse bridges such as Ashness were common particularly in upland areas where streams could easily flood during wet weather. They were designed to accommodate horses in single-file loaded with side-bags so there is often very little room for modern vehicles. Continue up the road to Surprise View and you will be rewarded with a vista which covers the whole length of Derwent Water.

Watendlath *above*

Situated at the end of an extremely narrow and twisting road from Derwent Water, this little hamlet is best approached on foot, either from Rosthwaite or Ashness – a route which also gives the opportunity of visiting the Lodore Falls on the way. Watendlath is the sort of place where ducks and geese seem to have as much right to the road as cars. A working farm often means that sheep-shearing, dipping and gathering take place under the nose of visitors. An ancient packhorse bridge crosses Watendlath Beck soon after it leaves the tarn. The tarn (left) is a great attraction for sightseers. Otherwise the hamlet consists of a farmhouse or two, one selling teas and another hiring out rowing boats for trout fishing. The entire area is in the ownership of the National Trust.

Crummock Water and Loweswater

Just across the fields from Buttermere is the southern end of Crummock Water. The view (above) shows the forbidding slopes of Melbreak which dominates the northern end of the lake. On the right – ablaze with the glow of dead bracken – is Rannerdale Knotts. The side valley of Rannerdale leads away from Crummock Water and is famous for the bluebells which carpet its slopes in spring. This strategic point was the site of a battle where Norman invaders were ambushed and routed by the English. The most northerly of the three interconnected lakes, Loweswater (right) is surrounded by attractive woodland; it is not surprising to learn that the name "Loweswater" is derived from the Old Norse words for "leafy lake".

Buttermere *left*

One of three connected lakes, Buttermere gives its name to the local village. Its remote valley can be reached either from the Newlands or Honister Passes. The village is located close to low-lying water meadows where cows were kept, giving Buttermere its name. The popular two-hour walk around the lake is an excellent introduction to the area. The village itself consists of little more than a farm and two hotels, The Bridge and The Fish Hotel. The latter became famous as the home of Mary Robinson, "The Beauty of Buttermere". Tourists would travel to the inn just to catch sight of her. The story of Mary Robinson is told in the book *The Maid of Buttermere* by Melvyn Bragg.

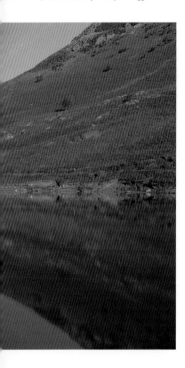

Braithwaite *above*

Tucked away at the foot of the Whinlatter Pass two miles west of Keswick, Braithwaite has some of the best walking in the Lakes on its doorstep. The spectacular backdrop of Grisedale Pike means that the village enjoys fine views of the Skiddaw massif. Bassenthwaite Lake is only a stone's throw away. The village is a regular starting point for the well-trodden 10-mile Coledale Round. The Coledale Beck adds greatly to the charm of the village, and the many bridges which cross and re-cross the beck make this an ideal spot for walkers.

Bassenthwaite

The village of Bassenthwaite (right) is located down a narrow side road one mile north-east of the lake (above). It nestles at the foot of Skiddaw, well away from the busy tourist centres. Apart from some bed and breakfast accommodation, Bassenthwaite gives the impression of being an ordinary village without the normal commercial features of a holiday area. This quiet unspoilt charm also extends to the neighbouring villages of Ireby and Uldale. Dash Beck rises "back o' Skiddaw" and cascades over Whitewater Dash; two miles downstream it flows past a grassy area and playground in the village. St John's church lies close to the main road, but another parish church, the ancient church of St Bega, is set in a romantic position surrounded by fields near the lakeshore just north of Mirehouse.

Lorton *right*

Situated in the lush Vale of Lorton, four miles from Cockermouth, the village is split into two settlements, High and Low Lorton. Neither settlement has an obvious centre, but both are attractive villages for the visitor to explore.

The original Jennings Brewery was founded in Lorton in 1828 and later moved to Cockermouth. The old brewery has now become the village hall. The splendid "Wordsworth yew" in the centre of the village next to the hall is the subject of the poem *Yew Trees* by William Wordsworth.

The unusual circular smokehouse is in the grounds of Lorton Park, a private house built in the 19th century. This listed building is used for smoking fish and ham. Lower Lorton is close to the Cocker and this fast-flowing stream was formerly used to power flour and linen mills.

Wythop Mill *above*

The charming hamlet of Wythop Mill, originally the site of a large cornmill, is located on the south side of the A66 between Keswick and Cockermouth. The name "Wythop" is thought to derive from the "wyth" or willow trees which grew profusely in the area. The mill dates from 1327 and was originally a fulling mill where cloth was treated to remove impurities and dirt; later it became a cornmill. Near Kelsick Farm are the ruins of St Margaret's chapel which date from 1673. In 1865 a new church was built on Sale Fell. The altar cross is made from a piece of wood recovered from the old church.

Western Lake District

This dramatic area is often referred to as the "wild west", a description that is not far off the mark. The remote valley of Wasdale and the area around Wast Water are about as far removed from "civilisation" as you are likely to get almost anywhere in England. Even the villages of this region, such as Boot and Wasdale Head, appear as tiny islands in a sea of wild and untamed countryside. Head towards the coast and the scenery changes completely especially around picturesque and historic towns such as St Bees and Ravenglass.

Wasdale

Close to the west coast of Cumbria, Wasdale is a hidden corner of the Lake District which, due to its remote location, has fewer visitors than other parts of the region. However, there is much for the visitor to enjoy – Wasdale is the home of Scafell Pike, England's highest mountain, its deepest lake, Wast Water and St Olaf's, its smallest church. The photograph (left) is the first view of Wast Water most visitors will see as they approach from the west. On the right of the photograph can be seen the rounded slopes of Scafell with Scafell Pike behind. Directly ahead are the sheer slopes of Great Gable. One of the most distinctive features of Wast Water is the Wasdale Screes which form a dramatic, mile-long wall on the south side of the lake. The overall drop amounts to nearly 2000ft (610m). The entire length of the Screes is riven by steep gullies, which offer challenging routes for the mountaineer.

The photograph (right) is of the packhorse bridge which lies behind the Wasdale Head Inn at the far end of the lake. This dramatic photograph (below) of Wasdale from Great Gable is taken from a vantage point close to the Westmorland Cairn, built in 1876 by two Westmorland brothers to mark what they regarded as the finest mountain viewpoint in the Lake District. It is hard to disagree. Lying a few hundred yards south, and out of sight of the summit of Great Gable, it clings to the mountain's rim above a startling drop.

Wasdale Head *above*

This tiny hamlet is the only clutch of buildings for miles around. It has a magnificent setting just north-east of Wast Water in an arena of dramatic mountains which include Scafell. The Wasdale Show in early October takes place in fields adjacent to the tiny St Olaf's church. The show features Herdwick sheep and a great variety of traditional sporting events take place, including hound-trailing.

Broughton-in-Furness *right*

On the southern tip of the national park, seven miles from Coniston, Broughton is a large village that manages successfully to tread the fine line of catering for its visitors, yet still retains the atmosphere of a local settlement. The handsome square at its heart is dominated by chestnut trees which are a beautiful sight in May with their flowering "candles". In the centre of the square is a pair of stocks and an obelisk. On the south side, the 17th-century town hall with its seven arches, clock and weather vane, make a superb home for the tourist information centre.

Broughton Mills (below), with its picturesque pub, is a tiny hamlet in an idyllic valley close to the Dunnerdale Fells, two miles north of Broughton. The small but beautiful Holy Innocents Church is well worth a visit.

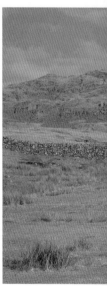

Eskdale *left*

The river Esk begins its journey at Great Moss, at the foot of Scafell Pike, and runs past the foot of Hardknott Pass, England's steepest road, down to the sea at Ravenglass. The course of the river takes it from high upland fells down into lush green pastures. The view shows Brotherilkeld Farm and the Upper Eskdale valley from the slopes of Harter Fell. Some of the giants of the Lake District's peaks are at the end of the valley – Scafell, Scafell Pike, Esk Pike, Bowfell and Crinkle Crags.

Hardknott Fort *below*

Located between Brotherilkeld Farm, and the Hardknott Pass, is the dramatically sited Roman fort of Hardknott. Founded under the Emperor Hadrian, the fort guarded the strategic Roman road which ran from the important harbour at Ravenglass on the coast, over the mountains to Ambleside. The fort has commanding views over the mountains and down to the sea.

Ennerdale Water *left*

The most westerly and remote of the lakes, Ennerdale Water and its surrounding fells seems far distant from the hubbub of tourism found in many of the lakes further east. Even in the height of summmer there are few visitors. This area's remote location is accentuated by the fact that there are few main roads: access to Ennerdale is by a network of tiny lanes. Even the lake itself is unique in Lakeland by having no paved road following any shoreline. Much of the land around the lake is owned by the Forestry Commission or the National Trust who have both organised a variety of walks around the lake.

The lake is dominated by the great cliffs of Pillar Fell, the mountain on the right of the photograph. Pillar Rock is a 500ft (892m) outcrop halfway up the summit. It was here in 1913 that the young George Mallory gained early experience ahead of his attempts to climb Everest during the inter-war years.

St Bees *above*

A popular destination four miles south of Whitehaven, this little town with its remarkable priory, its long sandy beach and fine sandstone headland contrasts with the mountain scenery inland. On clear days the coast of Scotland and the mountains of the Isle of Man can be seen across the Irish Sea. The four-mile long St Bees Head is a nature reserve. The 190-mile long coast-to-coast walk starts here and ends at Robin Hood's Bay in Yorkshire. The Priory Church of St Bega is renowned for its richly decorated Norman doorway and was established by Bega, an Irish nun who was shipwrecked here in the 9th century.

Ravenglass *below*

The only coastal village within the Lake District National Park, Ravenglass is situated a point on the estuary where the Irt, the Mite and the Esk rivers converge. The curv estuary channel close to the town provided a sheltered haven, one of the few natura harbours on the west coast between the river Dee in north Wales and the Solway F Ravenglass was originally a Roman supply port and there are significant remains of th old bath-house still standing. Today this characterful little village, with its cheerful fro gardens, makes for a worthwhile trip as well as being the terminal for the "La'al Ratt narrow gauge railway.

Muncaster Castle *left*

Just south of Ravenglass lies Munca Castle, which dominates the Esk Va for miles around. Described by Joh Ruskin as "Heaven's Gate" the cas has been home to the Pennington family for 800 years. Dating from t 13th century, the building began lif pele tower to deter marauding Sc and was gradually extended into a castle. In 1862, the fashionable arc Anthony Salvin was engaged to re the house and he ingeniously mer the tower and castle into one. Op the public, the castle is a treasure of art and antiques with an owl ce and famous gardens.

First published in 2010
by Myriad Books Limited,
35 Bishopsthorpe Road, London SE26 4PA

Photographs and text copyright © Val Corbett

Val Corbett has asserted her right under the Copyright, Designs and Patents Act 1998 to be identified as the author of this work.

ISBN 1 84746 349 5
EAN 978 1 84746 349 4

Designed by Jerry Goldie Graphic Design

Printed in China

www.myriadbooks.com